Contents

A Strange Dream _____ 7

Siddhartha is Born _____ 11

Within the Palace Walls _____ 15

The Giver or the Taker _____ 19

A Lonely Prince _____ 23

Beyond the Palace _____ 27

The First Sight _____ 30

The Second Sight _____ 33

A Rude Shock _____ 37

In Search of Truth _____ 41

A Princely Saint _____ 45

The Struggle Begins	48
A Kind Offering	52
The Awakening	56
The Path of Truth	60
Kindness to Animals	63
A Mother's Sorrow	68
Spreading Wisdom	71
An Evil Attempt	77
Defeated Assaults	80
Refuge in the Buddha	85
Touching Lives Forever	92

Foreword

Born a king, Siddhartha chose to live a humble life. He shared with others what he had discovered under the Bodhi tree. As Buddha, he led the people to live a life richer than all the riches of kings. All through his journey encompassing the life of a great and humble teacher, as a child, a prince, an ascetic and finally as a human being, the message we receive is – "Peace comes from within. Do not seek it without." This simple message has touched innumerable lives even 2500 years after his death. And, as we read on the tale of Buddha – The Awakened One, we realise that we "cannot travel the path until we become the path itself".

A Strange Dream

More than two thousand years ago, nestled beneath the foothills of the snowcapped Himalayas, was the kingdom of Kapilavastu. This kingdom was ruled by a wise and able ruler, King Suddhodana and his beautiful and gentle wife Queen Mahamaya. Under their rule, Kapilavastu prospered and the king, the queen and their people were very happy.

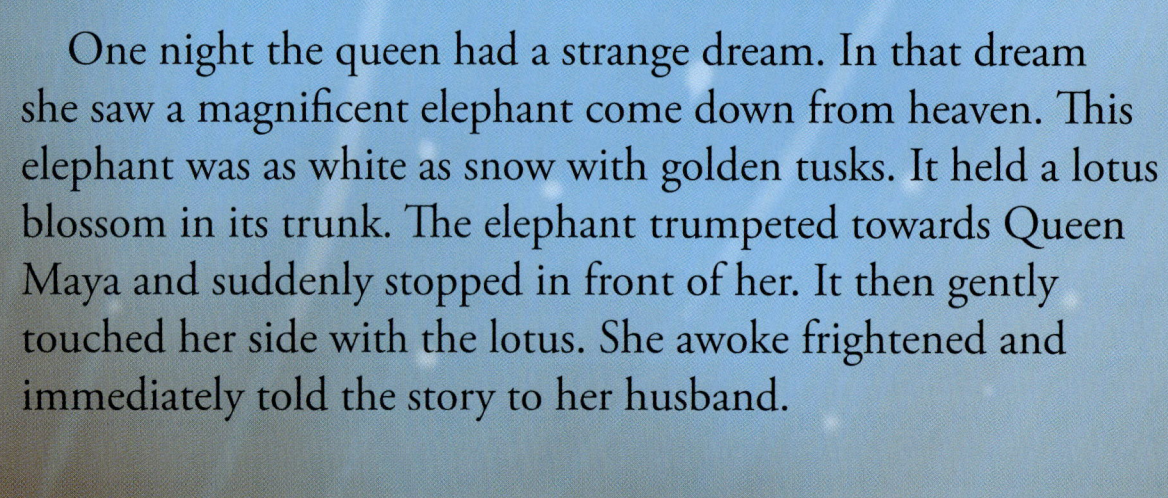

One night the queen had a strange dream. In that dream she saw a magnificent elephant come down from heaven. This elephant was as white as snow with golden tusks. It held a lotus blossom in its trunk. The elephant trumpeted towards Queen Maya and suddenly stopped in front of her. It then gently touched her side with the lotus. She awoke frightened and immediately told the story to her husband.

When the king heard this, he too thought that it was an unusual dream, and the next morning, he called all the wise men in his kingdom and asked them to interpret the dream.

"The queen shall bear a son," said the wisest of them all.

Siddhartha is Born

Indeed, as it had been foretold, the queen was to give birth to a child. Both the king and queen were filled with joy. The people too shared their happiness.

As the time of birth drew near, the queen set out in her decorated palanquin and left Kapilavastu to visit her home in Devadaha. On her way, she passed the beautiful Lumbini gardens and the queen, not being able to resist the scent of the sweet smelling flowers and lush green trees that surrounded the garden, stepped out. With the fresh feel of soft green grass under her feet, she walked and rested under an enormous sal tree.

It was a beautiful summer day and Queen Mahamaya was absorbed in her pleasant surroundings. Little did she know that she would not make it to Devadaha because, on that day in the month of May, as she lay under the huge Sal Tree she gave birth to a charming baby boy. As she cradled her baby in her arms, she was happier than she had ever been. She could not wait to present the new prince to the king as well as to the people. So, soon she started on her journey back home.

Queen Mahamaya and the little prince were welcomed with huge pomp and celebration into the kingdom. People blessed the child, crowds cheered and wise men rushed to see the prince's future.

"In him, there is greatness," prophesied the wisest of them all.

The King was overjoyed to hear that.

"He shall be a great king," exclaimed the wise man. "But, if he sees sickness, old age, death and a monk, he will leave the palace to become one himself."

This prophecy haunted the king's mind for days on end.

While the kingdom was still filled with merriment and pomp, misfortune struck the Kingdom and seven days after the baby was born, Queen Mahamaya died. The news shocked the entire kingdom. The people fell into a state of despair.

The king was grief-stricken at the death of his beloved wife. And he did not know who would raise his motherless child and help him to become the great king that he was destined to be.

Within the Palace Walls

"Siddhartha was born to rule the Kingdom of Kapilavastu and not to wander through the jungles like a hermit in search of truth and begging for food," thought the king.

So, he decided to prevent his son from ever becoming a monk. King Suddhodana came up with a brilliant solution. He would build a wall. He set out to build a great and vast wall that would surround all corners of the palace and would protect the prince from seeing any suffering or pain of the outside world. Within these walls, the king would make sure that there was no suffering or pain, for the future king to witness.

Within the great palace walls, he grew up, under the care of his mother's sister Prajapati with no knowledge of the world outside. Here, he learnt everything that a prince should.

As a young boy, Prince Siddhartha was thoughtful, considerate and kind. He was a remarkable student and his intelligence astounded everyone. What was even more remarkable was his gentle nature.

As a prince, Siddhartha excelled in the royal art of archery, yet he would never kill a bird or beast for pleasure.

One day, as he was walking through the royal garden delighting in the beauty and serenity of nature, he saw a bird which was injured. It had an arrow pierced through it.

Immediately, he felt pity for the bird and wondered who would have done something so cruel. It was badly wounded. He took out the arrow from the birds' body and tried to nurse it back.

Suddenly, Siddhartha's cousin, Devadatta came out of the bushes with a bow and arrow in his hand. "That bird is mine. I shot it and brought it down. Hand it over to me!" said the boy.

"You do not deserve it. You tried to kill it while I tried to save its life. It therefore belongs to me," said Siddhartha.

"No!" protested Devadatta. "That's not fair. Let's go to the court and ask the judge to decide."

At court, the boys narrated the story to the judge. The judge heard the story and decided to give the bird to Siddhartha.

"But I won it!" argued Devadatta.

"You shot an arrow at the bird and attempted to take its life, while Siddhartha saved it. Who do you think the bird would owe its life to — the giver or the taker?" asked the judge.

At that, Devadatta kept quiet and walked away.

Raised in the lap of luxury, Prince Siddhartha had everything he ever wanted. Yet, he was still unhappy. There was something missing in the princes' life and no matter how much the king tried to make him happy and protect him from all the suffering of the world, Prince Siddhartha was miserable.

As much as the prince loved spending time with nature in his wonderfully kept garden, he could not help feeling trapped. With childlike curiosity, Prince Siddhartha wondered what lay beyond the great and enormous palace walls. It was as if there was a voice from beyond the palace walls, calling out to him. As days passed, the voice became louder and louder.

King Suddhodana saw his son's unhappiness and, determined to keep him from becoming as monk, started looking for ways to prevent the prophecy from becoming true. Just then, an idea flashed in his mind. "Let's get him married," thought the king. At the age of sixteen, king Sudhodana sent his son to win the hand of the beautiful Yashodhara at her *swayamvara*.

At the *swayamvara*, Siddhartha was spectacular. He was a skilled fighter and archer and excelled in all the feats set up before the princes. Everyone was in awe of him. He won every match there and eventually won the hand of the beautiful princess Yashodhara.

But that too did not satisfy the prince's restless mind. The more Siddhartha saw all that he had inside the palace walls, the more he craved to go outside them.

Beyond the Palace

The king did everything he could to keep his son from venturing outside and seeing the suffering world. But despite all this, Siddhartha still longed to see what his father had prevented him from seeing all his life.

So one day, he asked for his father's permission to go outside the palace gates and King Sudhodana had no other choice but to allow him.

Siddhartha's mind was made up. He needed to see the world outside the palace walls, outside the comfort and luxury that his father had built for him.

The king ordered the people of the city to prepare for his son's visit. He gave strict instructions to the servants and the charioteer to take him only to places around the kingdom where he would not be able to see any suffering.

So, the prince set off on the journey that would change his life forever. As his chariot passed the streets of the Kingdom of Kapilavastu, he saw for the first time, the life of his people. He felt happy seeing them well.

The First Sight

But just as Channa was about to turn back, Siddhartha spotted something beyond the city boundaries and urged him to go further.

When they reached the spot, Siddhartha could not believe his eyes. He saw a man, but unlike one he had ever seen before! The man was bent and weak, his skin was wrinkled, his hair was white and he had no teeth. This man was so weak that he needed the support of a stick to be able to walk. This was something he had never seen before!

"Who is this man? What is wrong with him? Why is he so weak?" asked Siddhartha.

"He is old, master. He is bent with age," answered Channa.

"But why is he old?" questioned Siddhartha, not being able to understand what he saw.

"My Lord, we all are growing older every moment. It cannot be stopped," replied Channa.

On hearing this, the prince became very sad and depressed for he saw for the first time, old age.

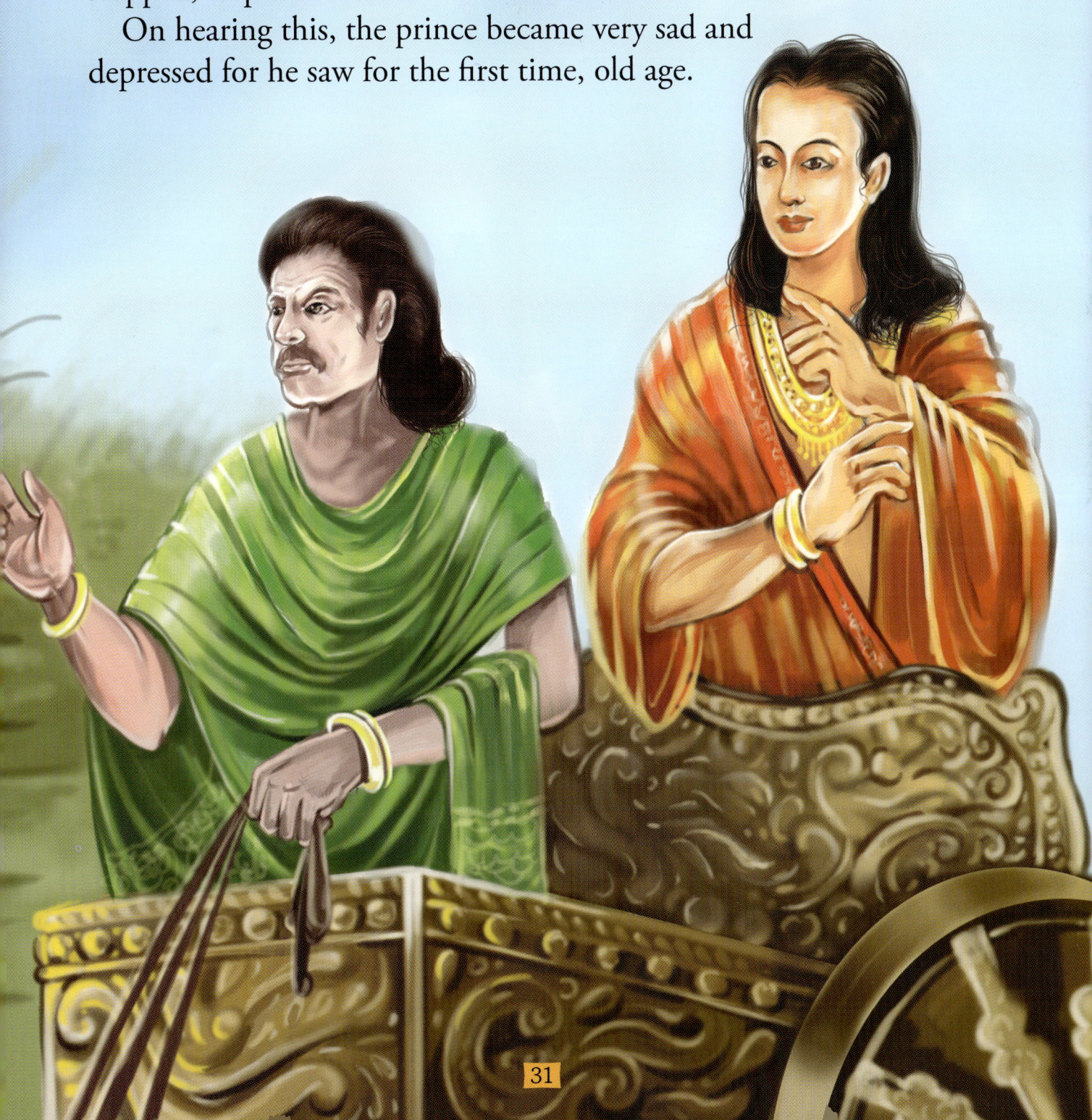

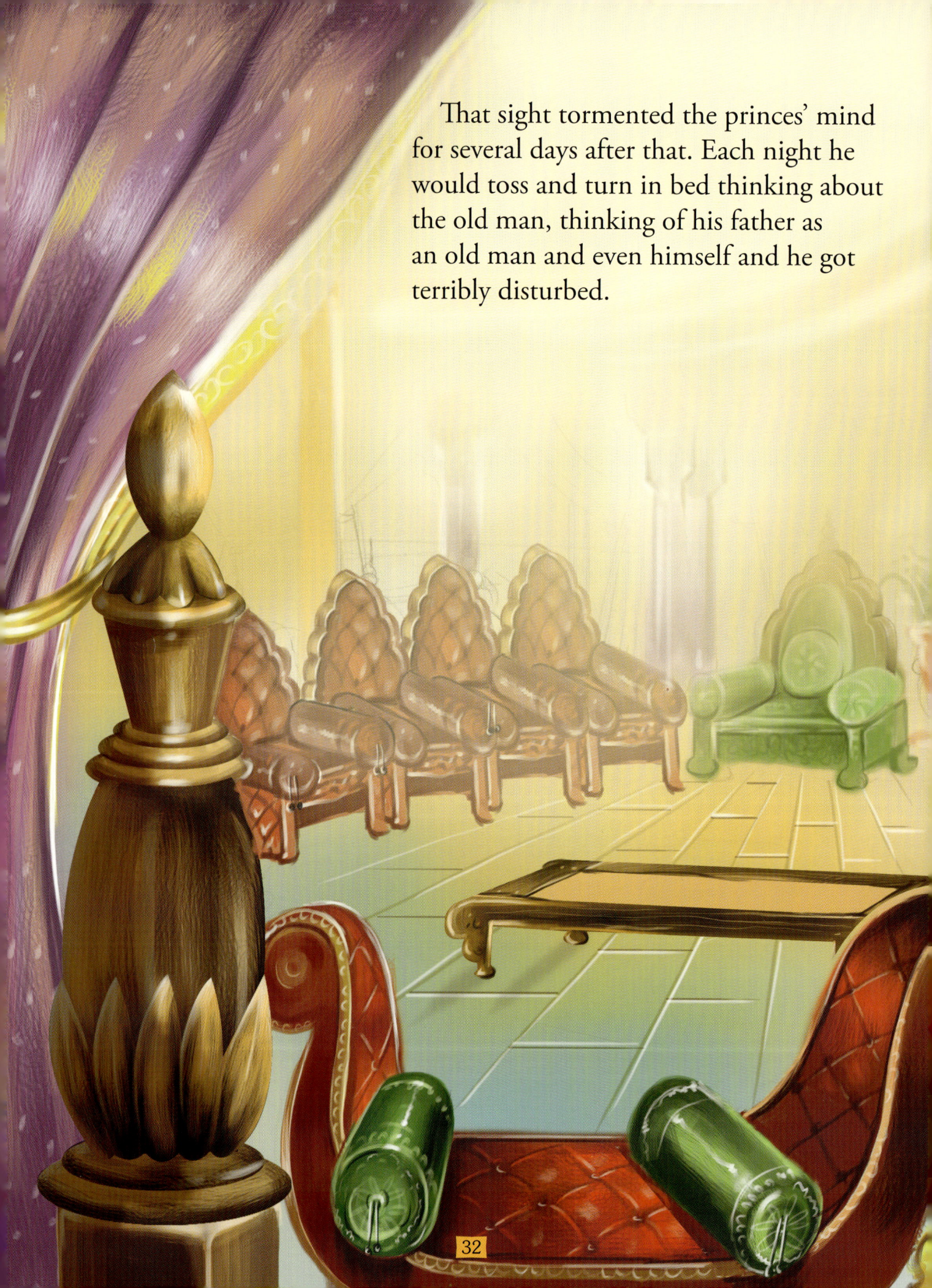

That sight tormented the princes' mind for several days after that. Each night he would toss and turn in bed thinking about the old man, thinking of his father as an old man and even himself and he got terribly disturbed.

The Second Sight

Finally, when he could take it no more, he went to the king, "Father, I want to go out to the city again."

The king unwillingly allowed his son to go out for the second time.

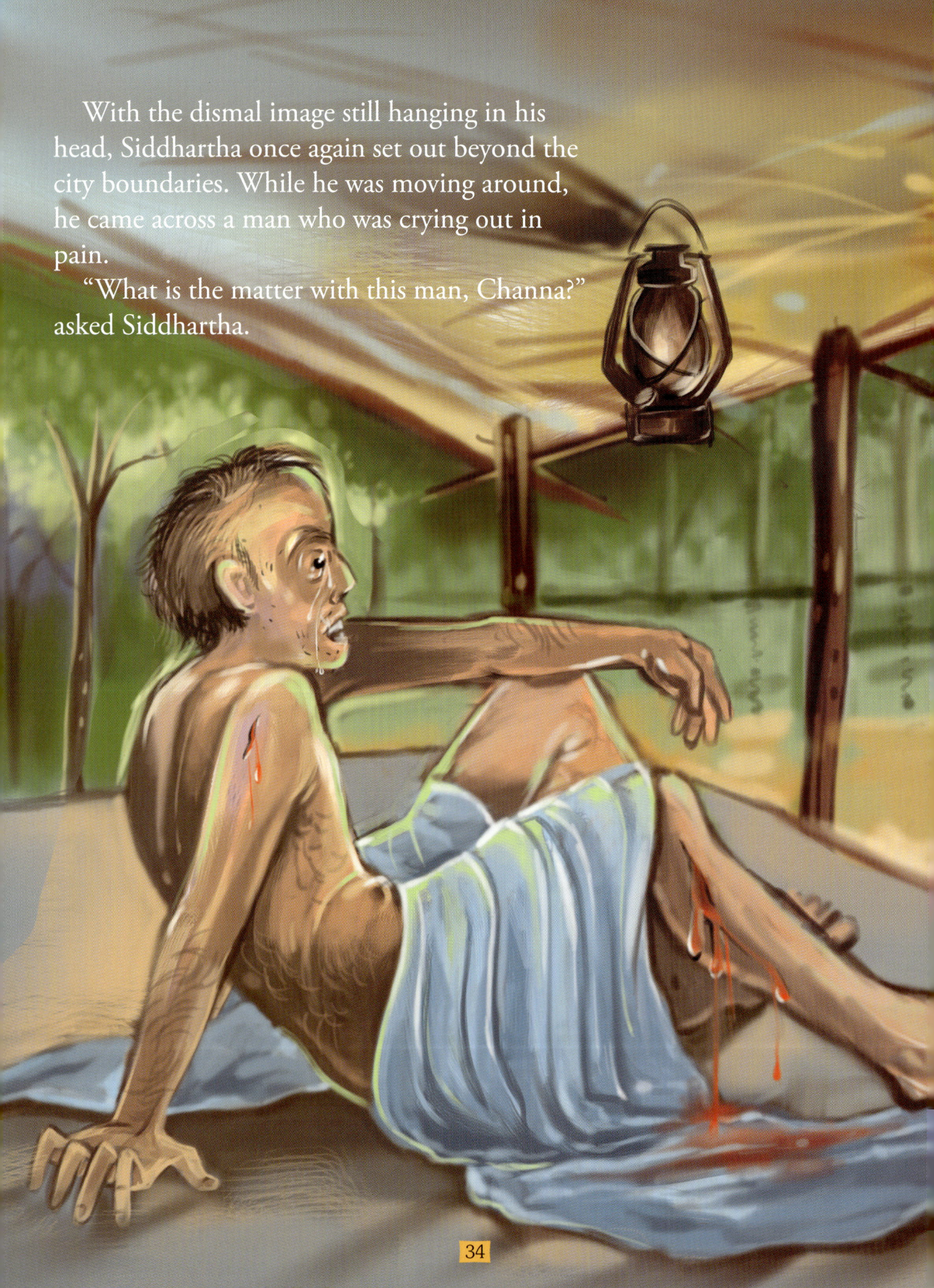

With the dismal image still hanging in his head, Siddhartha once again set out beyond the city boundaries. While he was moving around, he came across a man who was crying out in pain.

"What is the matter with this man, Channa?" asked Siddhartha.

"He is ill, my lord! He is crying in pain," answered Channa.

"But why is he ill? Why is he in pain? What has he done to deserve this?" questioned Siddhartha, not being able to bear seeing him in so much pain. "He didn't do anything, my lord. Surely you have seen sickness in your lifetime?" said Channa.

But Siddhartha had never seen sickness, or pain or old age. He understood then that sickness can come to anyone and could not bear the thought. He sympathised with the ailing man and wanted to help him but he did not know what to do.

A Rude Shock

Siddhartha kept thinking about the sickness and pain in the world for many days and was not satisfied with his life at all. Soon enough, he went out to the city again. After travelling for sometime, the prince saw a group of people carrying the body of a man.

"Why are they carrying that man, Channa," asked Siddhartha.

"He is dead, master," answered Channa.

"Is this the only dead man? Does everyone die, Channa?" asked the prince. "Will you also die? Will I die too?"

"Yes, my lord! Everyone who is born, has to die someday. No one can escape death," replied Channa.

The journey back was a quiet one. Siddhartha could not stop thinking about what he had seen. Just then, the prince saw a saint who was meditating under a tree. He found the saint different from all other people and asked Channa to stop the chariot.

"Who is that man, Channa? He looks so different from all the other men I have seen. He looks so calm and contented."

"He is a saint, my lord!" replied Channa.

"He has left his home and given up the pleasures of life to go in search of truth, peace of happiness," said Channa.

"What does he do Channa," asked surprised Siddhartha.
"Master, he goes from house to house for food and water and spends his time meditating and preaching to the people about peace and kindness."

Despite his father having sheltered him from all pain and ugliness, throughout his life, the young prince looked beyond the great palace walls and he saw sickness, misery and death and he felt immense compassion. He could not believe that there was so much misery in this world.

That same day, a son was born to him. And, while the whole kingdom was celebrating, he was lost in thought.

In Search of Truth

Upset, he kept tossing and turning the whole night. Siddhartha was born a leader to a great kingdom. But that fateful night, as he lay awake, under a starry sky, he realised that he could do better for his people, not as a prince or a king but as one amongst them - as a saint in search of truth.

He left his bed, looked at his wife and son once and bade them goodbye silently. And then he left, giving up his princely life and wealth to become a saint.

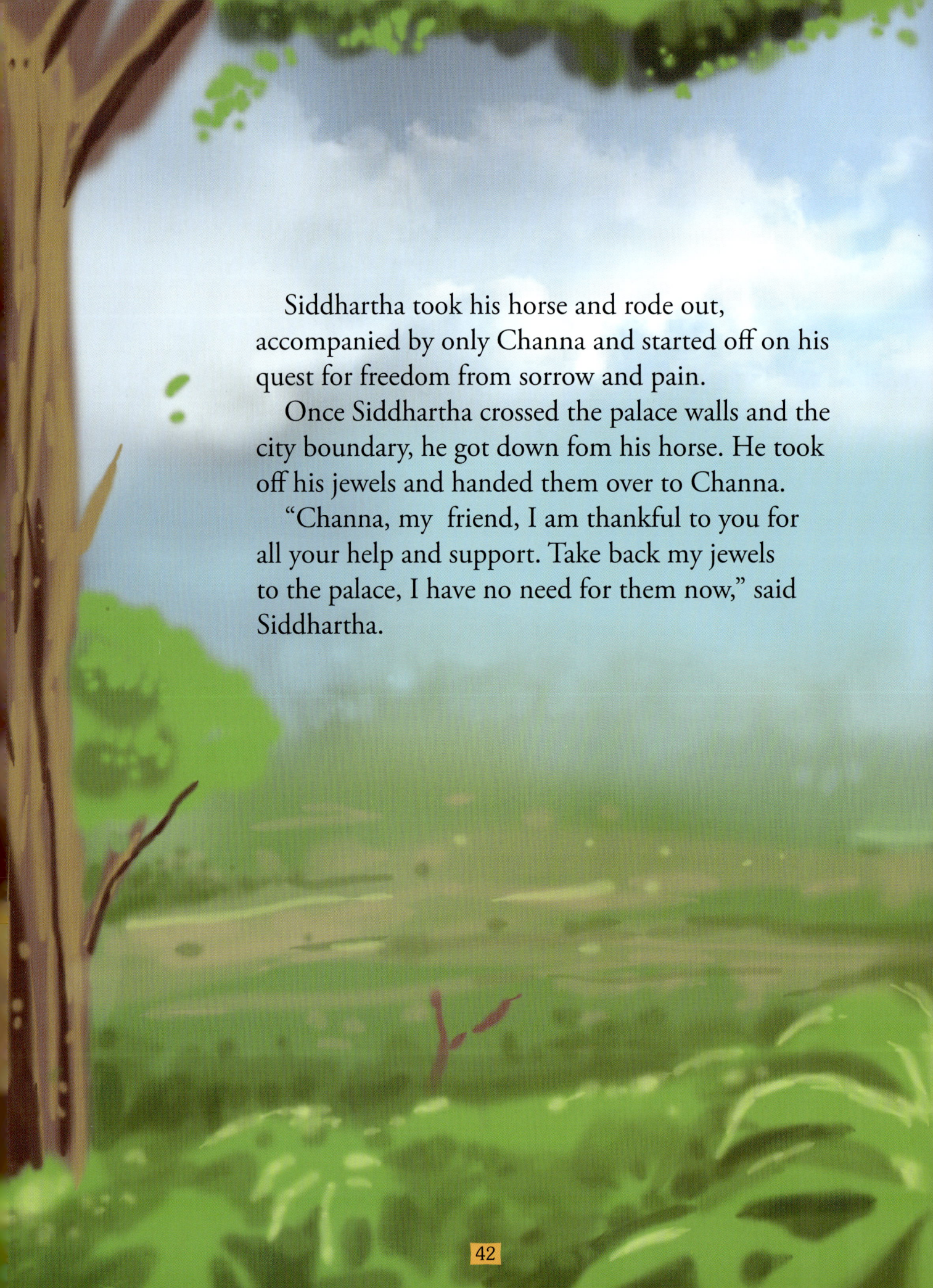

Siddhartha took his horse and rode out, accompanied by only Channa and started off on his quest for freedom from sorrow and pain.

Once Siddhartha crossed the palace walls and the city boundary, he got down fom his horse. He took off his jewels and handed them over to Channa.

"Channa, my friend, I am thankful to you for all your help and support. Take back my jewels to the palace, I have no need for them now," said Siddhartha.

Channa was very upset and was nearly in tears.

"Do not cry, Channa. Sooner or later we all have to part," said Siddhartha.

Channa obeyed his master and took all his belongings and left for the palace.

It was here that he began his spiritual journey. He cut off his long hair, exchanged his clothes with those of a beggars' and with a few humble possessions, he set out in search of the truth, to discover an end to suffering and to help others discover it too.

Thus abandoning the life of luxury, he began his journey in search of the path of truth.

A Princely Saint

No longer a prince, Siddhartha wandered from place to place. He went from house to house for food and water. After wandering for some time, he reached Rajagriha, the capital city of Maghda. One day while he was begging for food, he passed the palace gates and was spotted by King Bimbisara. The king saw something different about this saint. Although not dressed in princely attire, Siddhartha was still graceful. Surely, he could not get rid of his princely behaviour as easily as he could his clothes.

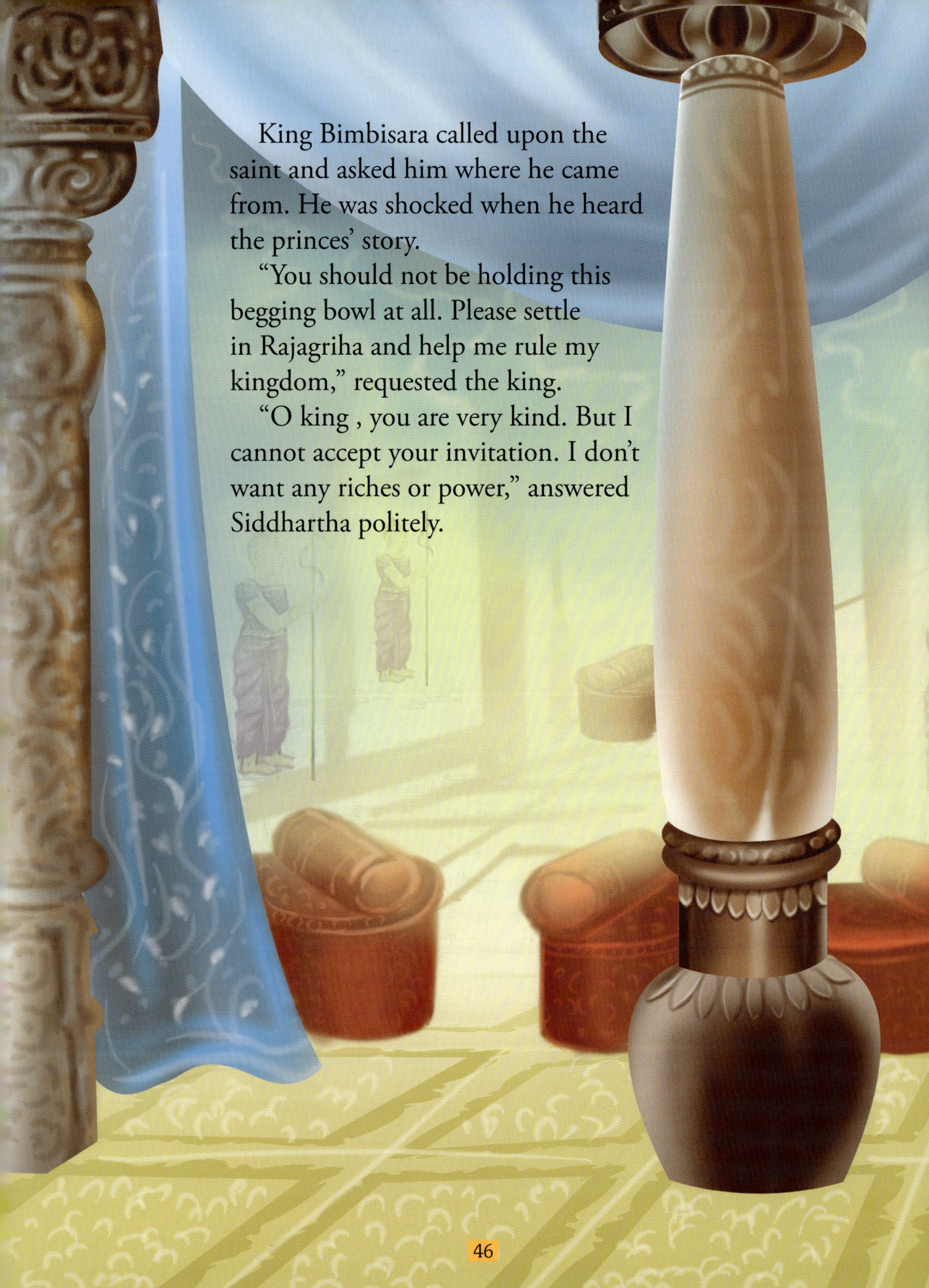

King Bimbisara called upon the saint and asked him where he came from. He was shocked when he heard the princes' story.

"You should not be holding this begging bowl at all. Please settle in Rajagriha and help me rule my kingdom," requested the king.

"O king, you are very kind. But I cannot accept your invitation. I don't want any riches or power," answered Siddhartha politely.

"I want to seek the path of truth. Life is full of sorrow and I want to find a way to end this," explained Siddhartha.

On hearing this, the king bowed to Siddhartha and wished him luck and success in his journey.

From Rajagriha, Siddhartha went in search of the great teachers for guidance. He travelled far and wide and he persevered under extreme conditions of hunger, thirst and weariness till he found himself within the thick jungles of Urubilva, located near the Gaya of today. There he studied with Arada and then with Udraka Ramaputra. He mastered everything that they taught him but his restless mind was not satisfied with their teachings.

So, he decided to travel more. He travelled till he reached the Nairangana river in Gaya. He crossed that river and reached a forest on the other side.

On reaching there, he met five hermits who lived out in the open, without a roof over their heads and with little food to eat. They were thin, their bodies were bent and frail and weak. He understood that they lived on meagre conditions.

"O holy men, why are you all living in such harsh conditions?" asked Siddhartha.

"There is so much suffering in the world around us. We feel that if we can learn to master pain, we can control our suffering," replied one of the hermits.

On hearing this, Siddhartha decided to join them in their practices to find the solution to end suffering.

Siddhartha began difficult and painful practices. He would sit in the scorching heat and meditate for hours. Even when his legs and back hurt, he would not move and continue sitting at the same spot come sunshine or rain. He lived on only water and fruits and became thinner and thinner with each passing day. His body became weak and lost its radiance. But he did not give up.

Instead, he started treating his body even more harshly. He stopped sleeping completely and would go on for days and nights meditating continuously.

The five ascetics were amazed by his determination. "This man is keen on his goal. He is sure to succeed in these practices. Let us wait on him," said one of them.

A Kind Offering

Many, many years passed like this. He was almost thirty-five now. It took him almost six years living with hardly any food, sleep, shelter and proper clothing to realise that this practice was not taking him any closer to the truth.

"I still feel as ignorant as I was when I left the palace," he thought. So he slowly pulled himself up and went to bathe in the river.

He was so weak that he could not even get up. Just as he reached the river, he stumbled and almost drowned in the river till he caught hold of a low branch of a tree and managed to pull himself out with great effort.

The following day, Siddhartha sat himself beneath a banyan tree. A woman by the name of Sujata, the wife of a herdsman from the village nearby went to him. She had recently given birth to her first child and was very happy. So she went and offered food to Siddhartha. She brought the finest milk and a delicious meal for him.

"Master, I have brought this food for you. Please accept this as a token of my reverence," said Sujata.

Siddhartha opened his eyes slowly and then he lifted the bowl to his lips and began to drink.

"Thank you for feeding me. Your offering has made me strong again. Now I am sure that I shall find the truth soon," replied Siddhartha.

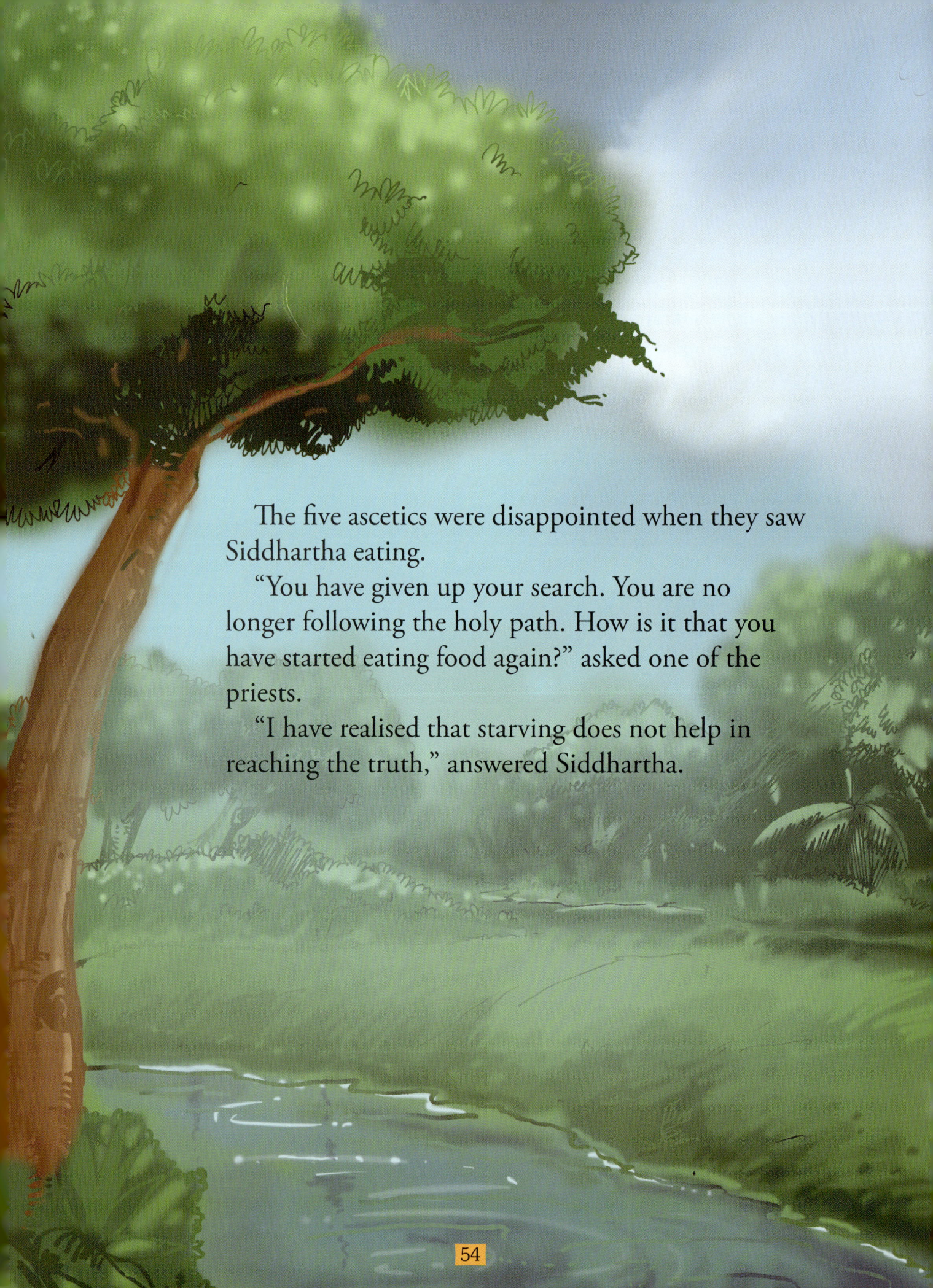

The five ascetics were disappointed when they saw Siddhartha eating.

"You have given up your search. You are no longer following the holy path. How is it that you have started eating food again?" asked one of the priests.

"I have realised that starving does not help in reaching the truth," answered Siddhartha.

"He wants the pleasures of life. He does not deserve our respect," said another ascetic.

"Let us leave him and travel to Varanasi for our practices," added another one.

Siddhartha now lived a lonely life. He understood that him leaving his luxurious life did not mean he needed to submit himself to self-torture. He needed to take care of himself and keep strong if he wanted to live and continue his search for truth.

The Awakening

After days of travelling, he reached a village near Gaya. There, he sat under a large banyan tree to meditate. The branches of the tree spread out in all directions sheltering him from all heat and cold for days on end. After intense meditation, he discovered the way within his own heart and mind. He discovered an end to suffering!

Siddhartha became the Buddha, the enlightened one, at the age of thirty-five.

The large banyan tree, now popularly known as the 'Bodhi Tree' protected him for seven weeks. Buddha was filled with happiness as his mind was free from ignorance and pain. He then went out into the world to teach others what he had discovered.

Buddha taught them the 'Four Noble Truths' which became the central teachings of Buddhism.

"There is suffering in this world. This suffering is caused by greed. If we free ourselves from greed, then only can we be free from suffering," said the Buddha.

"This is possible only if we follow the Middle Path." Buddha then went on to teach them all that he had discovered.

Indeed, he had become the 'Buddha' and the five ascetics, his devout disciples, came to be known as the Sanga.

The Path of Truth

After that, he returned to Urubilva and went to the house of Kashyapa, a worshipper of 'Agni', the god of fire. He asked him if he could stay in the room where the sacred fire was kept.

"The sacred fire is guarded by a serpent at night. It will bite you if you go near the fire," warned Kashyapa.

But Buddha insisted and the saint agreed to let Buddha spend night there.

Next morning, Kashyapa woke up worried.

"Let me go and look for him. He must be dead by now. Poor man!" thought Kashyapa.

He hurried into the room and to his surprise, he saw Buddha sitting peacefully, his face radiating in the light from the fire.

He rubbed his eyes in disbelief. He quickly rushed to Buddha's side and kneeled down.

"O great one! Teach me, for I am your follower," he exclaimed.

Kindness to Animals

News that King Bimbisara was organising a great *yajna* reached Buddha's ears and in keeping his promise, he decided to go there. On the way to Rajagriha, Buddha saw a herd of sheep. He then saw a lame lamb which was carried by a herdsman.

"Where are you going with this herd of sheep?" asked Buddha.

"These sheep belong to King Bimbisara. I am going to Rajagriha. These sheep are going to be sacrificed in the sacred fire," replied the herdsman.

Buddha accompanied the herdsman and headed towards Rajagriha.

When Buddha reached Rajagriha, King Bimbisara quickly sent his ministers to receive him.

"O great one! I am about to begin a *yajna*. I will be honoured if you and the great Kashyapa take part in it," requested Bimbisara.

"The killing of innocent animals is not a good deed at all. The way to happiness does not lie in *yajna*," answered Buddha.

"What do you think about the *yajna*, Kashyapa? You are a worshipper of fire," shocked, King Bimbisara asked Kashyapa.

"Neither the worship of fire nor the sacrifice of animals can make us free from sorrow. Buddha has shown me the right way," replied Kashyapa with full faith.

The king turned to Buddha.

"Let us hear your teachings" requested Bimbisara. Seeing his wisdom, people went to him and they all were delighted to hear his words. The king became a disciple of Buddha and took refuge in his teachings.

The Buddha had taught him the Truth and the path to inner peace. In return, he gifted Buddha and his Sanga the beautiful Venu Vana garden.

A Mother's Sorrow

People called him 'the Enlightened One.' They not only listened to his teachings but relied on him in times of sorrow and pain. And the Buddha had always helped them.

Once, in the town of Sarasvati, there lived a lady named Krisha Gautami whose son died. She went to the Buddha and said, "I was told that you could cure my son. Please bring my child back to life, master. He is my only child."

"Don't grieve my child and do as I say to you. Go, fetch me a few mustard seeds from any house where no death has taken place," replied Buddha.

"Mother, can you give me a few mustard seeds?" requested Krisha to a woman.

The woman went inside and brought the seeds. "Here you are," said the lady and handed over seeds to Krisha.

"Thank you mother. I trust this house has never known death," asked Krisha.

"We that are living in this house are few, compared with those that have died here," replied the lady.

She went on her quest from house to house but every house had known death. Disappointed, she went back to Buddha without the mustard seeds.

"Lord! I could not find a house where no death has taken place," said dejected Krisha.

"Nothing is permanent in this world, my child. All that is born must die one day. It is freedom from desire that frees us from sorrow," said Buddha, teaching wisdom to his followers.

Buddha's fame spread far and wide, to all corners of the earth, including his former kingdom, Kapilavastu. The king, old and weary of waiting for his son's return, called for him. It was his father's wish that Buddha would assume his role as the King of Kapilavastu. But Buddha had chosen his path. He had attained happiness and found truth. No amounts of wealth, power or position could overcome his decision.

Spreading Wisdom

The next morning, Buddha went from house to house to ask for alms. Upon seeing this, the king rushed to stop him.

"But this is how we live. This is our custom, father," replied Buddha.

"But you are not like them! You descended from kings," said the worried king.

"My descent is not from kings but from the Buddhas of old. They lived on alms only and went from door to door to collect food as shall I," answered Buddha.

During his stay there, people gathered at the palace to listen to Buddha and his teachings. He spoke softly and kindly to all those who had been waiting for him. But he noticed that Yashodhara was not present at the gathering.

"Where is Yashodhara?" Buddha asked one of the maids.

"My lord, she has refused to come," replied the maid.

"Ever since you left, she has been very unhappy. She wears very simple clothes, eats very less as you did. She has cut her hair as well," added the king.

"I want to meet her. I must heal the sorrow in her heart," said Buddha.

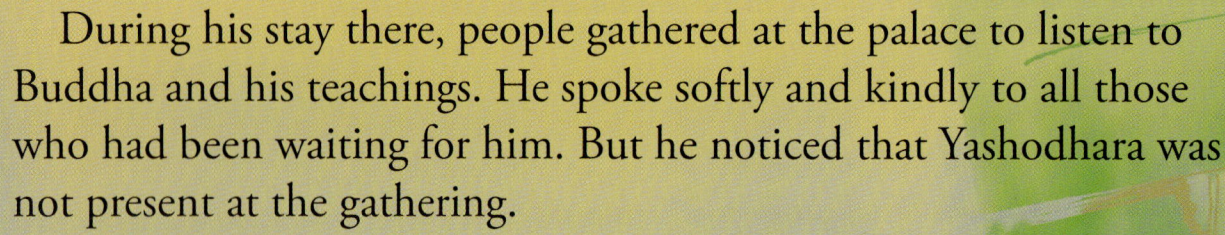

Buddha went to Yashodhara's chamber with some of his disciples. Yashodhara had not seen her husband for years and when she saw Buddha, she fell at his feet and wept. Buddha comforted her and taught her the right path.

One day, as Yashodhara was looking on at Buddha and his followers, her son, Rahula came to her. She took her son and showed the little boy his father. She sent Rahula to him to ask for his inheritance. She believed that since Buddha had renounced the throne, it should go to Rahula when his grandfather could not rule the kingdom anymore.

Rahula obediently went to his father and asked for his inheritance.

Rahula obediently went to his father and asked for his inheritance.

Buddha having lived that life- in the palace, luxuriously, getting all that he had wanted, knew that his son could not possibly find any happiness there. Instead, Buddha gave him spiritual enlightenment. Little Rahula was ordained into the Sangha as the first 'young monk'.

Soon after Rahula, Devdatta, Buddha's cousin, joined the Sanga.

An Evil Attempt

Devdatta was a cruel man and soon after he joined the Sanga, he grew to become jealous of Buddha.

Several times, he had even tried to trick Buddha into standing aside and letting him lead the Sanga. Once all his attempts had failed, he went to Prince Ajatshatru.

"What a great king you would make!" exclaimed Devdatta.

"Too bad your father is still alive. He is preventing you from meeting your destiny. What are you waiting for? Put him in prison and claim the throne!" poisoned the evil Devdatta.

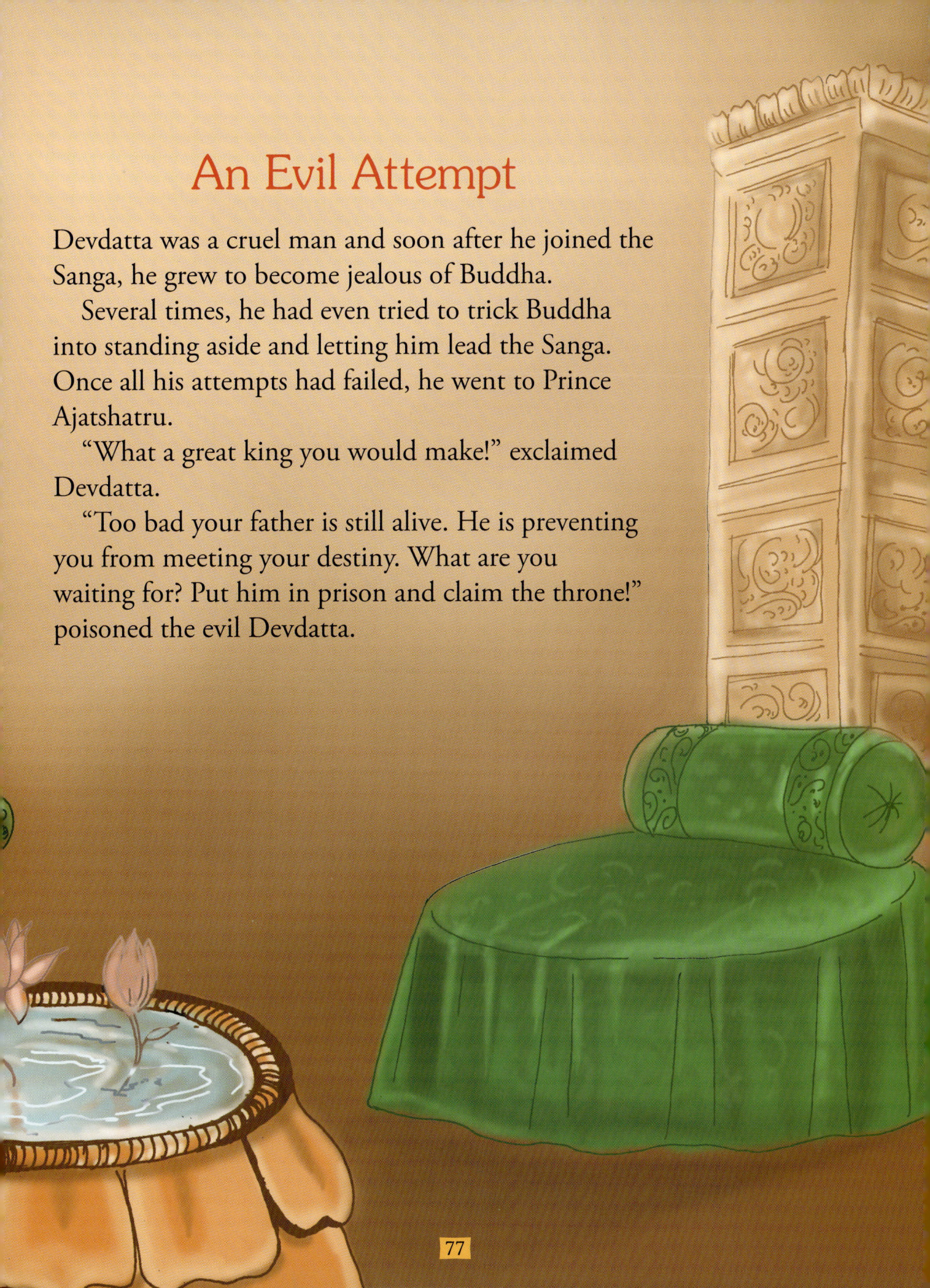

At once, the thougt had been planted in Prince Ajatshatru's mind. He put his father in prison and became king himself.

Satisfied with what he had done and thankful to Devdatta, he asked him, "Now that I am king, I can do whatever I please!" exclaimed Ajatshatru. "Tell me, what it is that you want from your new king, Devdatta?"

"I want your help to kill Buddha," replied Devdatta, silencing Ajatshatru.

Hesitantly, the prince agreed to help him.

Defeated Assaults

One day as Buddha sat with his Sangha, King Ajastshatru sent his men to kill Buddha. They rolled down a big stone from the steep hill just above the grove where Buddha and his disciples meditated.

When they saw the stone coming down at them, everyone panicked except for Buddha.

They ran for their lives. But Buddha did not move an inch. It rolled down quickly and just as it came closer to Buddha, it spilt into two pieces, each falling on either side of Buddha, causing him no harm!

After watching this miracle, many followers of Devdatta came to join the Sangha of Buddha

After this plan failed, Ajatshatru and Devdatta were very disappointed. So they thought of yet another plan to kill Buddha.

"Intoxicate the elephant Nalagiri, and then let him loose in the path of Buddha," ordered Ajatshatru.

The servants bowed to him and followed his order. Nalagiri was let loose in the streets.

"Run, run, Nalagiri is free. He has destroyed half of the town…so many people have been killed," shouted people.

There was panic all around.

When the disciples of Buddha saw this, they ran to the master to inform him about it.

"O great one! Let us hide somewhere. A wild elephant is coming this way," said one disciple.

"My child, don't worry. He is not going to harm us," answered Buddha calmly.

The wild elephant, Nalagiri, came running towards Buddha in a mad fury. Buddha just smiled at him and raised his hand. The mad elephant calmed down at once and knelt at Buddha's feet.

Refuge in the Buddha

One day, king Ajatshatru fell ill. He often suffered from one or the other ailment and he was a very unhappy man. His physician, Jivaka, was an old and wise man and he held a great respect for Buddha.

"Why do I always suffer from ailments, Jivaka. What's wrong with me?" asked Ajatshatru.

"My lord! Your ailment is not physical but spiritual. You should go to Buddha. Only he can cure you," said Jivaka.

"Please take me to him. Where can we find him?" asked Ajatshatru.

" In the Amravana, at Vaishali," replied Jivaka.

On reaching Amravana, Ajatshatru was very surprised to see how silent the place was. It was said that Buddha lived there with twelve hundred disciples. When King Ajatshatru heard this he could not believe his eyes. When he saw the assembly of men listening to Buddha in such silence, he was amazed.

As he stood there, listening to the Buddha's soothing words, he was influenced and encouraged by the calmness. It did not take long for him to join the Sanga as one of Buddha's disciples.

Touching Lives Forever

Indeed the Buddha taught an innumerable number of people about the Right Path. At the age of eighty, after long strenuous years of searching for the truth, and after teaching the people how to live with the truth, Buddha passed on. His soul abandoned his earthly body and reached 'Paninirvana', which is the death of someone who has attained complete awakening.

The Buddha not only touched people's lives during his lifetime but today, more than two thousand and five hundred years after his death, there are more Buddhist believers than there had ever been.

Through his sacrifices and struggles, the Buddhists of today have 'hope' and 'freedom' from suffering and pain. His dogma was simple — kindness, non-violence and resistance to templation. He lived by it.